BRITAIN IN OLD PHOTOGRAPHS

SOUTHAMPTON THEN & NOW

GW00384106

PENNY LE

The History Press

FOR THOMAS, WITH LOVE

First published 2010
Reprinted 2015

The History Press
The Mill, Brimscombe Port
Stroud, Gloucestershire, GL5 2QG
www.thehistorypress.co.uk

© Penny Legg, 2010

The right of Penny Legg to be identified as the Author
of this work has been asserted in accordance with the
Copyrights, Designs and Patents Act 1988.

British Library Cataloguing in Publication Data.
A catalogue record for this book is available from the British Library.

ISBN 978 0 7524 5693 5

Typesetting and origination by The History Press
Printed in China

CONTENTS

THE DUKE OF Wellington Pub in Bugle Street has been a public house since at least 1490. Originally known as The Brewe House and owned by a Flemish brewer Rowland Johnson, it later became the Shipwright's Arms. It acquired its current name after the magnificent Battle of Waterloo in 1815, when Wellington was a national hero. The top floor was lost in the Blitz in 1940 and rebuilt in 1961 at a cost of £34,407.

Today the Duke of Wellington stands proudly. It is now independently owned. The only original parts of the building left are the timbers to the ground floor, but, somehow, that does not seem to matter. The restoration works have been sympathetically done and the result stands out next to the twentieth century apartment building next door.

ACKNOWLEDGEMENTS

I hope I have remembered everyone who has helped me with this book. If I have forgotten to add your name, please accept my apologies and my sincere gratitude for your assistance.

My thanks to:

Joe Legg, my husband.
Nicola Guy, my Commissioning Editor at The History Press.
'Sir' Graham Hart, Sue Pheasant, 'Sir' David Priestly and the members of the
    Southampton Old Bowling Green.
Jimmy Marsh.
David and Nicky Basson.
Paul Stickler and Derek Stevens, Hampshire Constabulary History Society.
David Gibson, Deborah Mitchell, Joan Wood and the Southampton Philharmonic Choir.
Chris Hayles, *Southernlife*.
Nigel Wood and Lin Dowdell, Lingwood Netley Hospital Archive.
Pam Whittington.
Sue Woolgar, Sue Hill and Joanne Smith, Southampton City Archives.
Alan House, of the Hampshire Fire and Rescue Service, and all the officers at their
    Eastleigh Headquarters.
Robin Hancox and Eric Butler, Mayflower Theatre.
Jo and Barrie Short, The Old Farm House.
The Hampshire Constabulary Police Band led by Director of Music Major Jason
    Burcham RM and also the Deputy Director of Music, David Cole.
PC Martin (Dutchy) Holland and Sgt Snuggs, both based at Totton police station.
Sgt Colin Selby and Sgt Deborah Ashthorpe, Bitterne Police Station.
The officers at the City police station.
Jim Brown, Bitterne Historical Society.
Yvonne, Edward, Josephine and Henry Nevard.
Donna Saunders.
Zed Eric Malunat, Tasmania.
Pat Tarry, Southampton Sea Rangers.
Kate Fletcher and Zoe Redmill, Southampton Girl Guides.
Anthony Wilkinson, 2nd Southampton Scouts.
Allan Hailstone, photographer.
Daniele Pirola, Pirelli Historical Archives.
Julie Green.

Peter Oates, Southampton Canal Society.

Helen Zacharias.

Dean Smith, Marina Developments Ltd.

Mark Gibb, Head of Airside Operations, BAA Southampton.

David Hatchard.

Rachel Hudson, Operations Manager, Holiday Inn Southampton.

Maurice Mooney, Maintenance Manager, Holiday Inn Southampton.

Ralph and Douglas Easson, Easson's Coaches.

Colin Carter and the Fire Officers at St Mary's fire station.

Tessa Warburg.

Jan Brine.

David Trevor-Jones, Ocean Liner Society.

The parents and children of the 2nd Southampton Scout Group and 9th Southampton Scout Group.

The parents and children of the 1st Southampton South Guides and 6th Southampton Guides.

George Longhurst, 2nd Southampton Scout Group.

All of the staff at the Southampton Local Studies and Maritime Library.

The staff of the Southampton Park Hotel.

The Pirelli factory in 1922. The Pirelli Historical Archives have their earliest image of the factory, which made cables and was a huge employer in its heyday, dated as 1912. The giant West Quay shopping centre sits on the site today. *(Drawing courtesy of Daniela Pirola, Pirelli Historical Archives)*

INTRODUCTION

Condensing a pictorial history of Southampton into a few pages is quite a job! When you think about it, there are many aspects of the city and its suburbs that flash into our minds when pondering what makes up 'Southampton'. It may be the docks and the ever-growing size of the cruise ships, old buildings like the Tudor House Museum that bring a smile or remembering life as a Cub Scout long ago. When I was asked to put this book together I had visions of finding photographs of proud shopkeepers outside their premises and going off to find their modern-day equivalents, of using photographs of events of yesteryear and looking to see if they are still played out in the twenty-first century or of groups who met long ago and may still be meeting today. In the event, I found that recession had killed off a lot of the established small businesses. Many of the events I envisioned re-photographing take place in the summer and the period allocated for work on the book was the autumn and winter (and what a winter!) but it was the groups that came up trumps.

The year 2010 is an important year for several of Southampton's community groups, not to mention the airport. The Southampton Philharmonic Choir celebrates its 150th anniversary and its musical director, David Gibson, has been with the choir for twenty years. The Hampshire Constabulary Police Band will be 115 years young this year and the Girl Guide Association reaches its centenary. Over at Southampton airport, a hundred years of flying there will also be celebrated in 2010. I felt it was important to remember these anniversaries in this new book and so contacted all these various groups to see if they were interested in co-operating with me. They were, and the results are here for all to see.

Some of the photographs in *Southampton Then & Now* were particularly challenging to re-take, as the original vantage points are no longer available. Where this is the case I have taken the shot from the best angle I can, to give the nearest approximation of the original. Sometimes lighting was a problem. I am thinking particularly of the photograph of the Philharmonic Choir, taken in the very low light conditions of Winchester Cathedral. Some of the modern photographs required precision organisation, such as that needed for the Bitterne police cars photograph. Facilitated by the Hampshire Constabulary Historical Society, who also supplied the archive image I was reproducing, this necessitated an early morning and patient waiting for the sun to come up, as we needed to shut the road outside the police station for a few minutes and the early morning was far less busy than during the day. A full compliment of sleepy police officers at the end of a busy night shift turned up and the traffic slowing services of my husband Joe, who had stopped on his way to work to watch his wife's antics with the camera, were useful. The willing co-operation of early morning passing motorists, who had to wait while I took my shots, was appreciated.

Some people have heard about the book and contacted me to ask why I am bothering to follow in the footsteps of those who have already worked on similar books. To this I say that the city is forever changing. I have looked at the books already produced and notice the changes from even fairly recent editions. In this book you will see 'archive' photographs from as recently as 2006. I have included them in the book because of the differences the intervening time has brought. By the time this book is published the old City police station will have moved out of the Civic Centre into its new home at South Road and the bus garage in Portswood will have closed forever. The changes to the city will never cease and that is why books like *Southampton Then & Now* will continue to be produced, not just now, but also into the future.

I have endeavoured to give some structure to the photographs in the various chapters by linking them loosely together. Inevitably there is a little overlap in some subjects and I hope I will be forgiven for this. I hope too that those people I have disappointed by not including a photograph of their street will forgive me. Obtaining archive photographs was, in many cases, very difficult and it is not as easy as 'borrowing' a photograph from a book or website, as many people seem to think!

The last chapter takes us out of the city and just over the Eastleigh border to Netley. I have deliberately done this as the Royal Military Hospital and its village have such an interesting history, so very close to Southampton, that I felt it right to record just a little of it here.

I have listed the many people and organisations that have helped with this book on the acknowledgements page but there are certain individuals who deserve a mention here. The first is my husband, who must have been driven mad with my comings and goings with a camera in search of the perfect shot. Julie Green supplied many of the archive photographs, for which I am grateful. Derek Stevens and Paul Stickler of the Hampshire Constabulary Historical Society pulled out all the stops for me and I appreciate it. Alan House of the Hampshire Fire and Rescue Service was most helpful and Jimmy Marsh tramped many a mile around the city with me, often in the bitter cold and rain, to help me get my photographs.

I hope you enjoy this book. Southampton has come a long way since the Romans left at the end of the fourth century. Hamwih, the eighth-century fortified settlement, and Hamwic, its trading community on the river, has grown and spread. Its importance as an administrative centre was sealed by the ninth century and is remembered in its Old English name, *Ham-Tun*, meaning 'home' and a 'man-made enclosure'. From these early roots we have the city we know and love today.

Penny Legg, 2010

INTRODUCTION TO THE 2015 EDITION

After five years, there have been some changes to the Southampton skyline, so it is appropriate that I update the book. I thank my publishers for the opportunity to do so. Southampton suffered with the rest of the country in the recent recession and this is obvious still in some parts of the city. However, there are a lot of positives and improved road layouts, a busy cruise port, the continued growth of the Cultural Quarter and the new Sea City Museum are just some of the visible changes over the last few years. I hope you enjoy this updated edition of *Southampton Then & Now.*

Penny Legg, November 2014

1

LANDMARKS

JDOR HOUSE, SOUTHAMPTON.

SIR JOHN DAWTREY built the Tudor House in 1495. It stands in Bugle Street, in St Michael's Square. It was originally a family home, known as Huttofts or Lady Ann Guidotti's House, but over its long life has been, amongst other things, an artist's studio and home to a book-binding business. It is now a museum and has recently reopened to the public after a £1.9 million refurbishment, jointly funded by Southampton City Council, the Heritage Lottery Fund and English Heritage. The house and gardens now offer the visitor a peep into the lives of those who lived and worked there.

THE OLD PRISON, better known as God's House Tower, is a medieval building. It was originally named after St Julian's Hospital, known as God's House Hospital and founded in 1196, which was nearby. It was the town gaol and a bridewell between 1707 and 1855. The tower, built in 1417, was the first purpose-built artillery fortification in Britain. It housed gunpowder and shot on the ground floor and the firing platform was on the roof. This photograph was taken before 1907 as it shows the statue of Price Albert amongst the ivy going down the wall. This was by William Theed and was presented to the town by its five-times Mayor, Sir Frederick Perkins, in 1876. The statue was taken down in 1907, as it was feared that its dilapidated condition would offend Prince Albert's grandson, Kaiser William II, when he visited Southampton.

From 1963 until 26 September 2011, God's House Tower housed the Museum of Archaeology. Fifty years of city excavations were on display, covering Roman, Saxon and Medieval Southampton. The collection is a Designated Collection of National Importance and parts of it can be seen in the new Sea City Museum at the Civic Centre.

THIS 1907 PICTURE shows the fourteenth-century Wool House and the corner of the Royal Pier Hotel, which stood next to it until it was bombed during the Second World War. Medieval Southampton was an important wool trading port and this was one of several warehouses in the town. This one was used for storing wool, from the Cotswolds, prior to shipping. With the demise of the wool trade in the sixteenth century the Wool House was used to store alum for cloth dyeing, and, in the nineteenth century, it became a prison. The carvings made by French prisoners of war can still be seen on first-floor beams.

From 1961 until 2012, the old Wool House was home of the Southampton Maritime Museum and its fine maritime history collection. The first floor was devoted to the RMS *Titanic*, which sailed from Southampton on her ill-fated voyage in 1912. Many of the ship's crew came from the town. The *Titanic* exhibits are now housed in the Sea City Museum at the Civi Centre. Since the closure of the maritime museum, the Wool House has been used as an arts venue. Plans are now afoot to turn it into a microbrewery and public house.

THE TOWN QUAY'S Harbour Board Offices were built in 1925. An Act of Parliament in 1803 had set up the Harbour Commission, the forerunner of The Harbour Board, and it administered Southampton's pier and the docks. Built in Baroque style, the weather vane on the dome is distinctive.

Today the Town Quay is home to a 136-berth marina, with high-level security and nearby features such as boat repairs and services, fuel suppliers and a chandlery. The office buildings have been converted to a casino and luxury flats. The Hythe ferry still plies from the quay.

THE ROYAL VICTORIA Pier was opened by the Duchess of Kent and her daughter, Princess, later Queen, Victoria, on 8 July 1833. Becoming known as the Royal Pier, it was built to handle the growing number of small craft commuting between the town and the Isle of Wight. As it was made of wood, it required a lot of attention and it was rebuilt in 1891. It was reopened by Victoria's son, the Duke of Connaught, in 1892. The original gatehouse was demolished to make way for the railway line to the new docks. The tollhouse (pictured), complete with its distinctive dome, was built in 1930, to one side of the original site.

Having survived the Blitz, the pier's heyday was in the 1950s and 1960s, when the ballroom was open. However, all good things come to an end and the pier succumbed to fire in 1987. The tollhouse was derelict for some time but opened as a Thai restaurant in 2008. The Royal Pier is part of Southampton City Centre Master Plan and is earmarked for a £450 million development that will change the waterfront's landscape. A Development Agreement was signed in March 2014 and a planning application for mixed-use of the site is being formulated as this book goes to print. The Discover Southampton website states that: 'The waterfront will be revitalised; Mayflower Park will be recreated and extended, while speciality shops, offices, leisure venues, apartments and waterside attractions will be scattered along the shoreline. The park will become a high quality public space offering spectacular views of the water and pretty southern skies. These will be linked by pedestrian promenades and piers – a celebration of the city's maritime spirit.' Assuming that Planning Permission is granted, the nearby Red Funnel Ferry terminal will be relocated and the first work will start on the site in 2017.

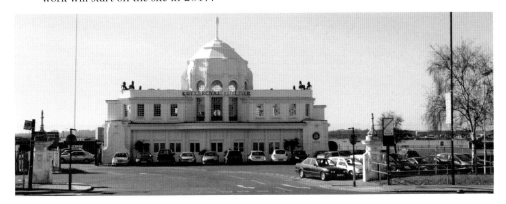

(Photograph courtesy of Zed Eric Malunat)

'Old City Wall, Southampton'

THIS VERY EARLY twentieth-century photograph shows the arcade at the Western Walls and, in the distance, the Blue Anchor Postern Gate. Before 1360 the walls were open, broken by merchants' houses. RF Renn, in his 1964 paper, 'The Southampton Arcade', published in *Medieval Archeology*, tells us that the blocking of the arches was undertaken in 1360 as a defensive measure. As there was little finance for this, the townsfolk decided to incorporate the houses into the defensive structure. Later, following the French takeover of the Isle of Wight, longbow and crossbow slits were made in the walls. Later still, gun ports were cut, for early, pole-mounted 'slim guns', which offered superior defensive coverage than that offered by the bows.

Today, the Western Walls still stand. The sea would have originally lapped at the walls but in the 1930s the land was reclaimed and now Southampton City Council has embedded a replica clinker-built cargo boat in front of the walls, as a reminder of the proximity of the water to the walls.

THIS EARLY 1930s photograph of the Bargate shows how congested the area was. As recently as 1910, buildings went right up to both sides of the Bargate. The Bargate Chambers at 1 High Street and the impressive offices of J.J. Burnett & Sons, whose estate agency, accountancy, insurance and mortgages, stock and share broking, architectural and surveying services, auctioneering and fire-assessing business was established in 1846, was at 2 High Street. By the time of this photograph, both businesses were gone and the tramline ran where they had stood.

All of the buildings either side of the Bargate were demolished in the 1930s to make way for the Bargate ring road. The west side of the ringroad was completed in 1938. Today the Bargate is an inland island proudly flying the Union Flag amidst a sea of pedestrians.

THIS IS THE view from the Bargate, Above Bar in 1910. The lions on either side of the Bargate are part of the story of Sir Bevois. There are reminders of his story all over the city. Part of the story says that Sir Bevois fell in love with the beautiful Josian on sight. The legend says that he was warned that he should not marry a woman who was not pure and his bride had also to be a King's daughter. Josian had been married to Yvor of Mombraunt for seven years but claimed that she was still a virgin. Sir Bevois believed her and carried her off. He left her sheltering in a cave, with her servant Boniface. While he was away two lions pounced on the luckless Boniface and ate him. However, as Josian was both a King's daughter and virtuous, they were unable to harm her and so sat quietly on either side of the cave, until the return of St Bevois, who recognised the danger they represented and so promptly slew them both.

By 2010 the twin pedestrian walkways through the Bargate had been filled in but the lions are still guarding the main arch. The whole area is now pedestrianised and the Bargate is a big tourist draw.

(Photograph courtesy Eric Butler, Mayflower Theatre)

THE EMPIRE THEATRE in Commercial Road opened on 22 December 1928, just as the 'talkies' were growing in popularity at the expense of live theatre entertainment and shortly before the Wall Street Crash, which sent shockwaves around the world and was felt in Southampton in the form of many job losses. The theatre was, at almost 2,300 seats, the largest theatre in Southern England. The local population flocked on open days to glimpse the luxurious interior, with walls lined with African marble, whilst backstage the actors enjoyed the hot and cold running water. The seats in the Grand Circle cost a fortune for the time, 5s 9d.

The Empire started to show films as well as live entertainment in 1933 and became the Gaumont in 1942. It continued to be a live venue and a cinema to 1987, when the last film was shown. In 1982 the building had become Grade II listed and in 1987 it opened as The Mayflower under the joint ownership of the Southampton City Council, Hampshire County Council and the Arts Council. Since then it has slowly evolved into a prestigious venue for touring West End shows, ballet, opera, comedy, pantomime and more, attracting some of the most famous names in show business. In 2012, the Mayflower celebrated its twenty-fifth anniversary by launching an appeal to fund an update to the main theatre entrance. The aim was to modernise the area and to provide more space in the foyer, a bigger box office and better street-level disabled access, all in keeping with its Grade II listing. The new foyer opened on Friday 30 August 2013 and the theatre took the opportunity to launch its new branding and logo at the same time.

THE PLAQUE ON the side of the clock tower in this late 1930s photograph of Bitterne Park Triangle states that it was 'bequeathed to the town of Southampton by Mrs Henrietta Bellenden Sayers, in evidence of her care for man and beast.' The tower was inaugurated in 1889 and was positioned originally on the corner of Above Bar and New Road. It was designed to be a drinking fountain for both men and horses, as well as a clock tower, hence the inscription.

The clock tower was moved to Bitterne in 1935 and still presides over the busy Triangle at its approach to Cobden Bridge.

2

PUBS AND HOTELS

THIS PICTURE OF the Old Farm House in Mount Pleasant is dated to about 1821. Then it stood in meadows on a pathway along the River Itchen. The farm was originally part of the Northam Manor. *(Image courtesy of Jo and Barrie Short)*

(Photograph courtesy of Jo and Barrie Short)

THE OLD FARMHOUSE pub, as it was at the turn of the twentieth century. The pub landlord and staff are in their best and the bicycle is the only mode of transport visible. The Old Farm House dates back to 1611, when it was rebuilt from a former building dating from before 1560. It is rumoured that Oliver Cromwell stayed there in the 1650s. The farmhouse became a public house in 1843, operated by Panton's Brewery, Wareham, on a 1000-year-old lease. Mrs Annette Eddy was the landlady in 1852. Scrase's Star Brewery took the pub over just before the end of the nineteenth century and Strong's Romsey Brewery later operated it.

Now a Grade II listed building, the pub has changed little but the 4x4 has replaced the humble bicycle. The pretty garden has made way for the car park and the demure long dark skirts worn by the ladies have given way to twenty-first century jeans. Barrie and Jo Short are now the owners and landlords.

THE STATION HOTEL, in Station Road, Totton, served by Ashby's Eling Brewery Ltd, as shown in this 1915 photograph. The brewery was founded in 1824. In 1856 Francis Ashby was listed as the owner. It was acquired by Strong and Co. Ltd in 1920. This was once the main thoroughfare into Totton's High Street. Note the railway station just up the road, which gave the hotel its name.

Today the Station Hotel has been converted into flats. Parked cars abound, although, with the coming of Commercial Road, it is no longer the main gateway into Totton and is now a backwater.

Palmerston Road Southampton

BUSTLING PALMERSTON ROAD was built in the 1840s but there has been a pub on the site of 1 Palmerston Road since the 1830s, when it was called the Joiner's Arms. The building was renamed the Eagle Hotel in the 1860s. Adjacent is Palmerston Park, with its statue of Lord Palmerston (1784-1865), who was born at Broadlands House, in Romsey.

The present building on the corner was erected in the 1920s when the Eagle Hotel was taken over by Strong's Romsey Brewery. It was bought by the Whitbread Group in 1969 and renamed the Hogshead and Eagle in 1993. In 2010 it was a sorry site as it was up for sale. Today, it is a bustling local convenience shop.

THE ROYAL HOTEL in Cumberland Place was one of the landmark sights opposite Watts Park. The hotel was originally two town houses, adapted to become one hotel. It is thought that Cumberland Place was named after George III's son, Ernest Augustus, the Duke of Cumberland, later Ernest Augustus I of Hanover (1771-1851), who came to Southampton in its spa-town heyday in the late eighteenth and early nineteenth centuries.

Now called the Southampton Park Hotel, operated by Forestdale Hotels, it is easy to see the hotel's residential heritage inside the building. When the hotel built its leisure centre a time capsule was found, dated 28 January 1862. Inside this was a document stating that Richard Hopkins Perkins, esquire, had built the original house and he was, 'for many years the principal auctioneer of this town'. The document goes on to give a fascinating insight into the building and the family who owned it: 'It was commenced building on the eighth day of April 1861 and finished about the same time of the following year and immediately afterwards occupied by Mr Perkins and Family. The Mayor of Southampton was Frederick Perkins esquire (third son of the above Richard Hopkins Perkins), who was also Mayor in the year 1860.'

THE DOLPHIN HOTEL in the High Street, Below Bar, has had a long career. Parts of the building date from 1250 and there is evidence of Elizabethan modifications. The exterior is graciously Georgian, with massive bow windows, said to be the biggest in England. It was formerly a post house. A daily postal coach ran between the hotel and the Swan With Two Necks in Lad Lane, London. The coach to Southampton left this very busy postal coach hub every morning at ten o'clock sharp. Queen Victoria stabled her horses here when she visited Osborne House, her home on the Isle of Wight. Jane Austen danced in the bow-fronted ballroom on her eighteenth birthday on 16 December 1793. In this photograph, Holyrood Church's spire stands proud in the background.

In November 2008 the Grade II listed hotel became a victim of the global recession and called in the administrators. A deal to build apartments in the hotel car park had fallen through, leaving the hotel in trouble, owing £4.7 million and needing to find a buyer. In August 2009, after being boarded up since May, it was reported that the hotel had been bought for an undisclosed sum. The scene has changed in the High Street following the bombing during the Second World War, which left Holyrood Church a ruin. Following an extensive refurbishment, the hotel was restored to its former glory and is now known as the Mercure Dolphin Hotel, Southampton. Once again, it is a bustling, comfortable hotel in the centre of the city.

(With kind permission of Southampton Library)

THE PILGRIM FATHER'S Memorial on the Western Esplanade, standing on reclaimed land where once the Southampton Waters rippled. The Memorial was unveiled in 1913 by the US Ambassador, Dr Walter Hines Page and commemorates the sailing of the *Mayflower* and the *Speedwell* from Southampton in 1620.

The trees have grown substantially in the intervening years. Bollards now line the esplanade. The hotel in the background, once the Skyway, is now the Holiday Inn. The whole area is in the process of undergoing extensive road development works as the city seeks to ease congestion around the docks area.

THIS SUPER PHOTOGRAPH of the South Western Hotel with a pig in the foreground dates from the turn of the twentieth century. The South Western Hotel was designed by architect John Norton and opened in 1872. The London & South Western Railway Co. owned it and the hotel extended over the platforms at Terminus Station. It was the hotel that many of the rich, ill-fated *Titanic* passengers stayed at prior to embarking the doomed vessel in 1912. During the Second World War the hotel was taken over by the Royal Navy and was known as HMS *Shrapnel*. After the war several companies used it, including the BBC and Cunard. The origin of the pig is not known.

In 2001 the Grade II listed building was redeveloped into luxury apartments. Now named South Western House, its spectacular staircase, which was copied on the *Titanic*, was restored and the marble and luxurious appointments of the grand entrance were retained. The road system outside South Western House has recently undergone a transformation in order to regulate traffic to the docks and through the city.

3

CHURCHES AND PARKS

HOLYROOD CHURCH WAS one of five churches that served the old city of Southampton. It was a Saxon church, built in 1320 on its present site, having stood originally in the centre of what is now the High Street since the eleventh century. Holyrood stood proud host to crusaders off to the Holy Land, soldiers setting out to the Battle of Agincourt and King Philip II of Spain, when he stopped at the church to pray before going to Winchester to marry Queen Mary in 1554.

On 30 November 1940 the Germans dropped bombs, which destroyed Holyrood. Life, as you can see from this wartime photograph, carried on and the police and local military were happy to see the mobile kitchen that was set up outside the ruins. In 1957 the church became a memorial to the Merchant Navy. A scheduled Ancient Monument, it was restored in 2004 as the elements had taken their toll on the unprotected interior. The Heritage Lottery Fund gave a grant of £670,000 for the repair of the tower and chancel and the installation of lighting. The Merchant Navy Association contributed another £5,000. Today the visitor can view memorial plaques and listen to recordings made by the Southampton Oral History Unit about how the church used to look. *(Photograph courtesy of the Hampshire Constabulary Historical Society)*

THE AREA NOW known as Freemantle was originally a large, privately owned estate. When this was broken up and sold off, the village of Freemantle was created. Christ Church, Freemantle is one of the oldest buildings in the parish and was consecrated in 1865. Church meetings first took place in the bailiff's house in 1856 and the foundation stone for the current church was laid in 1861. Architect William White (1825-1900) designed the church. White also designed several other churches in the area, including St Mary's in Woolston. Originally built without a spire, this was added in 1875. Freemantle had been a district of Millbrook but in 1866 it became a parish in its own right.

The Revd Brian Cox has presided over Christ Church since 2006. The church no longer stands at the junction of quiet roads, as twenty-first century traffic now makes Paynes Road and Waterloo Road busy. It took some time of patient waiting to take a photograph without motor vehicles intruding into the shot!

Jesus Chapel, (1620 A.D.) Pear Tree Church, N⁰ Southampton. 1039.

JESUS CHAPEL, PEARTREE, was built in 1618 from recycled Roman stone taken from Bitterne Manor House, a farmhouse relict of part of the old Roman Clausentum, or Roman station, which is believed to have been a supply and storage depot in the area. The chapel was the first post-Reformation church to be built in England. The building faces the open spaces of Peartree Common, supposedly named after the pear tree that stands there. Traditionally it is said that the first tree was planted by Queen Elizabeth I but there is little to substantiate this. The current tree was planted in 1951.

To take the overflow of inhabitants as the local area expanded, the Church of St Mark was built in 1860. John Silvester was the vicar at Jesus Chapel and moved from there to St Mark's, after a brief spell abroad. His cousin, Thomas Lewis, took over the living at Peartree. Now the chapel stands picturesquely, mellow in its old age. The cemetery is now closed to further burials but many local families are represented on its headstones. Jesus Chapel is still an active church within the local community.

29

SOUTHAMPTON'S MOTHER CHURCH, St Mary's, dates back to Saxon times, although it has been rebuilt several times on the site. There was a complete rebuild between 1876-84, to the designs set out by architect George Edmund Street (1824-1881). The Foundation Stone was laid in the presence of the Prince of Wales, later King Edward VII. Originally built without a steeple, this was added in 1913. As with so much of Southampton, St Mary's was badly damaged in the Blitz in 1940.

The church was rebuilt and re-consecrated in 1956, by Romilly B. Craze, who retained the 1913 200ft tall spire. St Mary's Church football team was the forerunner of the present-day Southampton Football Club, known as 'The Saints'. St Mary's Church Deanery Football Club merged with the football club at the St Mary's Church of England Young Men's Association to form what evolved into St Mary's FC and later Southampton St Mary's FC. After winning the Southern League in 1896-97 the name was further amended to Southampton FC. The rest is history.

40   SOUTHAMPTON. — St-Andrew's Church. — I.L.

THE GOTHIC SPLENDOUR of St Andrew's Scottish Presbyterian Church, on the corner of Brunswick Place and Dorset Avenue, was built in 1852-3, the brainchild of Southampton architects William Hinves and Alfred Bedborough. The church had strong links with shipping and related companies, particularly with P&O, whose superintendent engineer, Andrew Lamb, donated the site. Brunswick Place was named after Caroline of Brunswick, wife of George IV.

St Andrew's Church, although Grade II listed, was demolished in 1998 following its redundancy after merging with the Avenue United Reform Church. Today the imposing Royal Bank of Scotland Brunswick Gate building dominates the site, thus retaining the area's Scottish links.

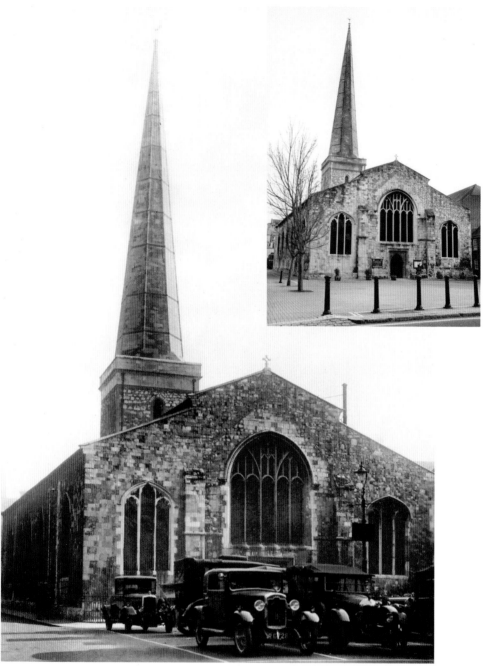

ST MICHAEL'S CHURCH is Southampton's oldest surviving church, parts of which date from about 1070. The spire was added later, in the fifteenth century, subsequently reconstructed and then, in 1877, extended to 165ft as a guide to shipping coming in to Southampton. Urgent repairs were found necessary to the spire in 1922 and it consequently spent many months encased in scaffolding while the corroded iron rings in the masonry were replaced.

Miraculously escaping unscathed from the 1940 bombing, St Andrew's Church now looks after the parishes of St Michael's, Holyrood, St Lawrence and St John.

WATTS PARK, ALSO known as West Park, is a pleasant, leafy open space, very pretty in the spring; it is named after hymn writer Sir Isaac Watts who was born in Southampton in 1674 (died 1748). The Civic Centre clock bells ring Watts' hymn 'Oh God, our help in ages past' every four hours. The park is home to the Cenotaph war memorial, designed by Sir Edwin Lutyens (1869-1944) and unveiled in 1920 with the names of 2008 dead from the First World War. It was the template for the Whitehall Cenotaph in London and constructed of Portland stone. In this early photograph, the stone is still pristine.

Today, after more than ninety years, the stone has mellowed and darkened with age. Towering office blocks dominate the background but little has changed otherwise. The names of the fallen are now inscribed on glass panels, as the original carved names in stone were wearing away due to exposure to the elements. It is still a reflective spot, even though the road through the park is just feet away.

SOUTHAMPTON. QUEEN'S PARK AND GORDON MEMORIAL.

THIS PRETTY IMAGE of the Queen's Park and Gordon Memorial also shows the Georgian row of houses named Queen's Terrace in the background. Queen's Park has an interesting history. Owned by Queen's College, Oxford, the land was called Porter's Meadow. It was Lammas Land (1 August was traditionally observed as harvest festival, when bread baked from the first wheat crop was blessed), being used as common land for half the year and reverting to the College for the rest of the year. Southampton City Council leased it in the nineteenth century and it became known as Queen's Park. The memorial was put up in 1885 after the death of General Gordon (1833-1885) at Khartoum during the Crimean War.

After many years as little more than a leafy roundabout, with traffic thundering by on all sides, the road has now been re-routed and so no longer flows past Queen's Terrace. Some of the terrace's residential buildings have disappeared, replaced by office blocks. General Gordon still presides over the park, which is a pretty spot amidst the hustle and bustle of a busy area of town.

(With kind permission of Southampton Library)

THIS HOUSE WAS built in 1818 by Thomas Ridding, Southampton's Town Clerk. After being badly damaged during the war, it was demolished in 1946, just five years after this picture was taken. Southampton Zoo, part of the giant Chipperfield operation which ran circuses and safari parks up and down the country, was then established on the site. It was used as a holding unit for animals on transfer between safari parks and operated between 1963 and 1985 at a site on Southampton Common. The Hawthorns Urban Wildlife Centre, seen below, now occupies the site of the former zoo. The Centre documents the natural history in the area, which includes the internationally rare great crested newt.

(Photograph courtesy of the Southampton Archives Office)

THE COWHERD'S PUBLIC house on Southampton Common has changed little since it was built on the site of another building in 1762. The cowherd in charge of the welfare of the animals grazing on the Common lived there. In 1774 Edward Dyett was appointed the cowherd. He was also a brewer who sold his beer on the premises, thus establishing the tradition, which continues to this day. The premises became a public house in 1789 and they became known officially as the Southampton Arms; however, locals persistently referred to them as the 'Cowherd's house' and the name finally stuck in the 1870s.

The Cowherd's was refurbished several times in the late twentieth century and remains a very popular spot on the Common. Today it is almost impossible to see behind the array of parked cars in its car park and the view of tarmac and managed paths from the spot in the earlier picture is not as romantic.

(Photograph courtesy of Allan Hailstone – www.flickr.com/photos/allhails)

ALLAN HAILSTONE TOOK this photograph of The New Docks, from Mayflower Park, on 16 August 1959. The ship is the SS *Nevasa*, built by the British India Steam Navigation Co. Ltd in 1956. She was a troop carrier, built during the days of National Service. Sadly, only six years later, National Service was scrapped and, in any case, more personnel were being transferred by air than by sea. The ship was converted into an educational cruise ship and took school children to European ports. She ended her days in a breaker's yard in Taiwan in 1975.

The scene has little changed in the intervening years, and ships such as the *Braemar*, operated by Fred Olsen Cruises, still draw an interested audience.

THE OCEAN VILLAGE site from the air: this photograph, which is used with the kind permission of Southampton Library, shows the site in 1930, when it was known as 'Inner and Outer Dock'.

The Jolly Jack Tar statue in Ocean Village, seen below in 2005, was a cheery sight on the corner of Asturias Way and Channel Way, near the Royal Yacht Club premises. Now the plinth is left, but the statue is gone. Research has proved fruitless in finding out where or why it disappeared. Prosperity seems to have moved on with the hit of the recession and the loss of this statue, and that of the Canute Pavilion, seems to say it all for the residential area in this part of the village.

(Photograph courtesy of Julie Green)

4

FROM A TO B

BOAC OPERATED FLYING boat services to Japan, Australia and South Africa from its Berth 50, Eastern Docks, Marine Air Terminal, between 1948 and 1950. It had operated from the Western Docks before the Second World War when Southampton was the centre of the Empire Air Mail Scheme. At the outbreak of war, the company had moved its operations out of the strategically important, and therefore enemy-targeted Southampton, to Poole in Dorset. After the war it returned and began building the new terminal in 1947. Hythe, Saxon (*Hithe*) for 'good landing place' is believed to have had a ferry running to and from what we now call Southampton since 400 AD. The excellent Hythe Ferry website (www. Hytheferry.co.uk) tells us that in 1683 Dr Speed wrote that to be exempt from the toll of 4*d* each time he landed, a boatload of stones had to be deposited against the Southampton town walls, within the piles, every six months. In 1832 stout 'Wherries' began their duties; physically carrying passengers ashore so that they did not get their feet wet when the ferry landed at Hythe Hard. Today the ferry plies between Hythe Pier and Town Quay, and everybody keeps their feet dry.

THE FLOATING BRIDGE operated across the Itchen linking the two sides of the river. It effectively put the proud Itchen ferrymen out of business. For centuries they had made a lucrative trade in rowing passengers between the two banks. The Itchen Bridge Co. came into being in 1833 and by 1836 was taking passengers between Woolston and Southampton in just four minutes.

The Itchen Toll Bridge was built in 1977 and ended the reign of the floating bridge. It opened at the beginning of June and ten days later the last floating bridge crossed the river.

(Photograph courtesy of Marina Developments Ltd)

THIS PHOTOGRAPH OF Roll On-Roll Off ferries was taken in 1969 in the heyday of the Southampton port's ferry business. Roll On-Roll Off ferries to and from France and the Channel Islands were a common sight for decades. However, endless industrial disputes made time-critical companies such as Channel ferries reluctant to stay in Southampton and the advent of the shorter crossing from Portsmouth sounded the death knell for Southampton as a cross-Channel ferry port.

It is hard to believe that Ocean Village Marina is the same place that bustled with cross-Channel ferries for decades. Now owned by Marina Developments Ltd, it has changed significantly. Dean Smith, Head of Sales and Marketing for MDL, puts it thus: 'Established in the 1970s, MDL Marinas have grown to become Europe's largest marina group, currently operating 21 major marinas and boatyards and managing over 7,000 marina berths. Our very first marina was on the River Thames and was followed by, amongst others, Hythe Village Marina and Ocean Village Marina. Ocean Village Marina was redeveloped by Dean & Dyball during the late 1980s and acquired by MDL soon after. Ocean Villages' fantastic location has seen the marina host international sailing events and provide one of a very few waterfront accesses for the city, ensuring that the former port lives on and continues its maritime links, albeit that the boats are now a little smaller.'

(Photograph courtesy of Julie Green)

BY 2003 LARGE, luxury apartment blocks were being put up in Ocean Village and it was the trendy place to be. This block overlooks the Ocean Village Marina, with its bobbing yachts.

In 2010 the apartment buildings are finished and sold off. There is a fashionable air to the Village by the water, with swish restaurants on the ground floors of some of the tower blocks.

THIS WAS THE first Easson's coach, a Model T Ford. Douglas Easson (died 1924), the grandfather of the firm's twenty-first century owners, Ralph and Douglas Easson, started the business in 1920. The first service ran from Butts Road to the Floating Bridge and later expanded to run from Hedge End. The coach had solid tyres at the back and pneumatic at the front. The sign on the bonnet reads 'D.J. Easson' – Douglas James. The coach spent each night sharing the stables with the horses, behind the Chamberlyne Arms in North East Road. Here the Model T is parked in what is now Spring Road, on the corner of Wodehouse Road. The road has not been made up and there are few houses in the background.

Ralph and Douglas Easson have now retired and so Eassons Coaches are no more. Comparing the archive street to the modern one, the houses in the background are now more numerous and the road has been made up and has road markings.

Bitterne Station.

BITTERNE ROAD RAILWAY station was originally planned to go through the centre of Bitterne but was eventually built a mile away, at the bottom of Lances Hill. The line is on the main Southampton to Portsmouth coastal link. The footbridge was erected in 1903. Elizabeth Mentor (1861-1941) & Co. published this postcard. The company opened for business as photographers in Southampton at No. 9 Oxford Street in 1891 and worked in Southampton until 1907. Thus this picture was taken between 1903, when the bridge was erected, and 1907.

The station name changed in 1896 and it is now known as plain Bitterne railway station. Little has changed except the car park is now made up and has car parking spaces outlined on it. The goods yard closed in 1959 and the signal box was taken out of service in 1966.

(Photograph above courtesy of Ralph and Douglas Easson)

THE EASSON'S CONCRETE garage in Wodehouse Road, Sholing, was finished in 1948, when this photograph was taken, at which time there were five coaches in the fleet. Before 1948 there was a corrugated-iron garage on the site. It adjoined the family's garden as the house was next door, between the filling station at the end of the road and the coach garage. The coach washdown area was originally at the back of the petrol station but was more convenient next to the garage, so the garden was sacrificed.

Today, although the garage is still standing, Eassons Coaches are gone. The site looks forlorn, a beacon to a bygone area.

(Photograph courtesy of Mark Gibb, Head of Airside Operations, BAA Southampton)

A CLASS 442 Wessex Electric five-coach train waits at Southampton Parkway's platform one, London bound. These trains were introduced in 1987 when electrification of the line west of Bournemouth to Weymouth was complete. They replaced slam-door stock. Red lamp-posts were a trademark of the Network Southeast period. In the background is the airport. To the right of the picture stands the old air traffic control tower, with its replacement to the left of the new terminal building.

What a difference sixteen years makes! The bright red lamp-posts are a shadow of their former vibrant selves and the Wessex Electric has been replaced by a new Class 444, German built, Desiro. The railway station now has an airside car park and the airport presents a trimmer appearance. Flybe, evolved from Jersey European Airways, is the major operator at the airport.

(Photograph courtesy of David Hatchard)

SOUTHAMPTON PARKWAY STATION opened in 1966 as Southampton/Eastleigh Airport station. This late 1980s photograph shows the old Network Southeast signage on the platform. The train is a four-coach electric multiple unit, first introduced for the London to Brighton services in the early 1960s in British Railways corporate blue and grey livery from the 1970s/'80s. They went on to serve across the entire southern region of British Railways. The footbridge is a pre-cast concrete product of the Southern Railway Concrete Works, which used to be situated in Exeter. These were very common all over the south's railways from the 1930s.

In 2010 the station has changed considerably. Gone is the Network Southeast colour scheme, having been replaced by South West Trains' in 1994. The station building sports a new concave roof and the sparkling new footbridge at the London end of the platform opened a mere few months ago. The train has changed a little too! The one pictured is a Cross Country Trains Class 220 Voyager, top speed 125mph, introduced on the Bournemouth to Manchester route by Virgin Trains in 2001.

THIS SUPER SHOT, taken in Oatbank Road, Woolston, is a snapshot of 1950s life. The coaches were small and comfortable and the advertising hoardings bring us some familiar names – Heinz and HP Sauce are still with us today. The gentleman in the background wears a working-man's flat cap. Keep your eye on the streetlight...

Nowadays the streetlight is all that is recognizable about the area. Gone are the advertising hoardings and now there is an unnamed road along the car park that has been built in their place. In the background is the slope of the Itchen Bridge, which dominates the whole area.

(Image above courtesy of Ralph and Douglas Easson)

UNLOADING FLOWERS FROM Guernsey, above, at the airport during the 1950s.

Much had changed by the time of the 1995 shot (opposite above) of the new taxiway and apron at Southampton Airport, taken from the steps on neighbouring Southampton Airport Parkway railway station. The airport, which celebrates its centenary in 2010, began life when Eric Rowland Moon brought his homemade aeroplane, *Moonbeam II*, to the North Stoneham meadows on which the airport now stands. He succeeded in flying his aircraft there and history was made. Twenty-two years later the airport was built, with a grass landing strip, which was to be the cause of much controversy. The *Southern Evening Echo* (12 February 1962) reported that a de Havilland Heron belonging to Jersey Airlines had got bogged down in the soft mud at the airport and had to be towed out of trouble. This led to Cambrian Airways withdrawing all services from the airport until it acquired a hard runway. The airport did not get this until 1965.

The *Southern Evening Echo* (23 February 1965) recorded that by 1957 a peak of 112,354 passengers had gone through the airport terminal, either in transit or on arrival. In 1995 there was a major update of the facilities at the airport, part of which was the new taxiway and apron here.

Today the railway steps are still there but the view has moved on. Now a huge stores building stands obscuring the new taxiway, but, if you are lucky, you can normally glimpse an aircraft from this point.

(Image courtesy of Mark Gibb, Head of Airside Operations, BAA Southampton)

THIS WAS THE original Easson's petrol station on the corner of Wodehouse and Spring Roads in Sholing. The photograph shows founder Douglas Eassons' older brother Ernie, with his older sister Marcia and their younger brother Don. In the background is their maternal grandfather, Mr Humby, the present owners' great-grandfather. The petrol station opened in 1921/22 with gallon barrels of Pratts' petrol stored in the shed, which was poured through a funnel into the cars when they came to fill up. This image was taken soon after the introduction of the new petrol pumps, in 1928. This freed the garage to house the Model T Ford coach. To the right is the edge of the newly built family house. Douglas James died suddenly in 1924, leaving his widow, Ellen Louise to bring up four children between the ages of six months and fifteen years. She did that and ran the business too.

Today the filling station site is the home of Spring Road Tyres. The original building has not changed very much, although the big wooden doors at the entrance have gone, replaced with windows.

5

SOUTHAMPTON'S PEOPLE

MEET EDITH MARSH and her family on their first day trip from Southampton. The children were born just before or during the war and had never left the city. This day was a never-to-be-forgotten outing to Bournemouth. Little Jimmy, second from the right, wandered off, excited and wide-eyed, and caused a panic, but was found, so all was well. *(Photograph courtesy of James Marsh)*

FOLLOWING THE SUCCESS of the Boy Scouts, Robert Baden-Powell was asked to design a similar programme for girls. He enlisted the help of his sister Agnes and together they wrote *How Girls Can Help Build Up the Empire*, upon which the Girl Guide movement was

based when it came into being in 1910. 1st Southampton South Girl Guides was delighted to present a Queen's Guide Award at St Mark's Church, in Archers Road.

Today the uniforms have changed, as has the name of the award, but the 1st Southampton South Girl Guides are still going strong, meeting on Tuesdays at Bannister School in Archers Road. This is District Commissioner Southampton South Claire Sheikh, and Emma Catt, 2010 candidate for the Baden Powell Award, which has replaced the Queen's Guide Award, along with Zoe Redmill, Guide Leader.

(Photograph courtesy of Southern Daily Echo)

THINKING DAY, 22 February, in 1984 was a special day for Pat Tarry. Thinking Day celebrates the birthdays of the founders of the Girl Guide Association, Robert Baden-Powell and his wife Olave, and encourages Girl Guides to think of others around the world. It was on this date that the silver Laurel Award was presented to Southampton Sea Ranger Leader Pat Tarry ('Skip') for outstanding services to the Guide movement. She was taken completely unawares as the award was kept secret until it was presented by District Commissioner Stella Neaves. 'I hadn't a clue at the time!' she says.

Pat and Stella today are both Laurel Award winners (note Stella's on her lapel). Pat went on to become District Commissioner, County and then Regional Boating Advisor before retiring recently. 2010 was the centenary year of Girl Guiding, which was marked with events and celebrations all over the world.

(Photograph courtesy of Zoe Redmill)

1ST SOUTHAMPTON SOUTH Guides in the early 1960s in front of the old St Mark's Church in Archers Road. This was just down the road from The Dell football stadium and was built in 1891. It was demolished in 1983.

1st Southampton South and 6th Southampton Guides in the twenty-first century. Gone are the smart, military-style uniforms and now Guides choose from an official range of clothing. The proceeds from the sale of St Mark's Church went towards adapting the church hall for services.

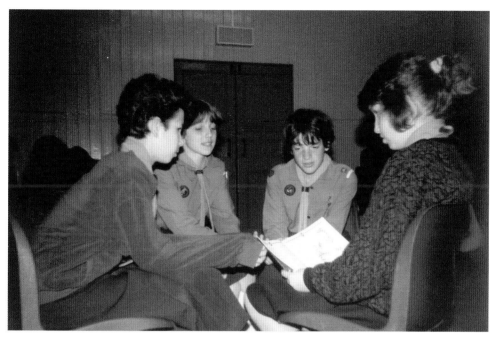

(Photograph courtesy of Zoe Rednill)

IN THE 1980s Guide uniforms had changed but the brightly coloured necker was still in evidence, as seen here as 4th Southampton South Guides try to read maps. This group met at St Denys but closed down ten years ago.

Today map reading is still on the agenda but livelier pursuits are more popular. This game is so fast it is over almost before it begins! The idea is not to break the circle but to drag your group around the gym without knocking over the upturned bin in the centre. The moment the bin goes flying (flying is the word!) the game is over. It is fast and provokes huge amounts of laughter.

(Photograph courtesy of Anthony Wilkinson)

THE 2ND SOUTHAMPTON Boy Scouts in 1944 on the steps of St James' Ground. Note the super hats and long shorts, neckers and woggles. Robert Baden-Powell started the Scout movement after adapting his book *Aids to Scouting* for younger readers. In 1907 the Scouts were born after the first Scout camp, to Brownsea Island, led to his 1908 book, *Scouting for Boys*.

Today the original steps in St James' Recreation Ground have been taken out and replaced with a grassy bank. The house seen in the 1944 shot is still standing and makes a suitable backdrop on a wet March morning. The 2nd Southampton City Scouts, based in Shirley (which celebrated its centenary in 2009) no longer wear long shorts and sport bare knees. Now practicality is the order of the day and so the hats have gone too. Here Akela Anthony Wilkinson recreates the 1944 shot with his cubs.

THE 2ND SOUTHAMPTON City Scouts in 1957 at St George's Day Parade. Mike Ford proudly holds the flag at the front of a well-behaved Scout troop. Akela Mary Kernick looks over Mike's head at the camera and to her right is her assistant Cub Scout Leader Pam Hatchard. To Pam's right is Akela Babs Longhurst and her Assistant Cub Scout Leader Margaret 'Mig' Penfold.

The 2nd Southampton (blue neckers) and 9th Southampton (blue and red neckers) at the Southampton St George's Day Parade, 2010. Scouts nowadays can come in both varieties: boys and girls. The Scouts were asked to bring along St George's Flags and many had whistles and musical instruments they had made themselves. The resulting procession, from Kingsland Square to the Central Hall, was extremely noisy! Scouts from all over Southampton joined the annual parade and church service, which celebrates England's patron saint.

(Photograph above courtesy of Anthony Wilkinson)

THE SPORTS CENTRE in 1963 and a proud 2nd Southampton Scout Football Team have just won the Boy Scouts Football Award. In the background is Senior Scout Leader Bill Smith. Holding the award is Barry Jackson.

Today, the Scouts are still playing for the same award, although it has now been mounted on a wooden back plate that is full of the names of the winning teams in the fifty-one years since the first photograph was taken.

THIS IS A glimpse into the world of the Southampton City police station local intelligence office. Note the lack of mod-cons. The clock on the wall, the light fittings and the typewriter are the high-tech devices of the early 1960s. Even the wooden chair the officer is sitting on at the typewriter looks as if it was from a bygone era! Can you see a telephone?

(Photograph above courtesy of the Hampshire Constabulary Historical Society)

Today, not just the room but the whole police station has closed, to make way for the new Sea City Museum, which opened on 10 April 2012, to mark the centenary of the departure of the RMS *Titanic* from the city. The police station moved to a new, purpose-built facility nearby.

THIS PHOTOGRAPH DATES from the early 1970s and is of PC David Hales, Southampton Central sub-divisional motorcyclist. It was taken in front of the Southampton City police station and PC Hales has parked his motorcycle on the path between the main road and the side of the main station building. PC Hales used his motorcycle for escort duties guarding the daily Bank of England bullion run. In 1938 it was decided to open a branch of the Bank of

(Photograph courtesy of the Hampshire Constabulary Historical Society)

England in Southampton. On 29 April 1940 the Bank of England opened its branch in the High Street and this became a useful centre in the South of England for the issue and payment of notes, for receiving and shipping gold and currency and was used as a gold depository. The branch closed on 28 November 1986, on its removal to Winchester.

Meet PC Martin 'Dutchy' Holland, with his BMW R 1200 RT mighty machine, capable of over 130mph. The bike weighs 229kgs and, as Dutchy says, 'You can probably fit the old bike into this one's panniers!' Dutchy picked up his nickname twenty-five years ago at his first police station in Cosham. With a surname like Holland, it could be nothing else! Dutchy was a full-time motorcycle officer from 1994 until December 2003, after which he decided to divide his time between patrol cars and motorcycles. What is so striking about this photograph when comparing it to the 1970s version is that now high visibility and safety are paramount. Both the motorbike and the officer can be seen at a great distance and they wear armoured protective clothing, which is a far cry from that issued to PC Hales. In the background the listed building has not changed but the volume of cars parked in the area has. The whole area is now one snaking car park.

(Photograph courtesy of Hampshire Constabulary Historical Society)

THIS SHOT WAS taken in about 1967 at Bitterne police station, just as the panda cars were going out on patrol. Notice the awkwardly situated lamp-post.

The first thing that everyone involved in retaking the 1960s shot noticed was that the lamp-post on the corner of the road had gone! Nowadays the reflective nature of both clothing and today's high-powered patrol car paintwork is what stands out – just as it should do.

(Photograph courtesy of David Basson)

THE BAND OF the Hampshire Constabulary celebrates its 115th birthday at the end of 2010. The band began as the Southampton Borough Police Band in 1895 and became its present formation upon the amalgamation of the Portsmouth, Southampton and Hampshire Police Forces in April 1967. In 1937 it was an all-male affair.

Nowadays the ladies have joined the gentlemen in the band. It is based at the Police Training Headquarters at Netley and its members are drawn from serving and retired officers, augmented by civilian musicians. The band raises money for charity with their military-style approach, covering marches and classical pieces through to contemporary works. Major John Burchem RM is the current bandmaster. A pianist and cornet player, he trained at the Royal Marines School of Music in Deal. On promotion to Major in 2007 he was appointed as a Staff Officer at the Royal Marines Band Service and took up his appointment as Director of Music of the Band of the Hampshire Constabulary soon after. The band celebrated its 2010 birthday with a trip to visit the St Lucia police band.

Photograph courtesy of Sue Pheasant, Secretary, Southampton Old Bowling Green)

THE SOUTHAMPTON OLD Bowling Green claims the Green to be the oldest Bowling Green in the world, being established 'prior to 1299' according to the Club's research. The lawns were originally laid in 1187 as a close for the Warden of nearby God's House Hospital. Much of the early history of the Southampton Old Bowling Green was not recorded, as noted by Sir Bert Baker and his team, who compiled the history of the first 700 years of the Green in 1999. This, they noted, may have been because of the severe penalties for playing the game if you were one of the 'inferior people', who were prohibited from playing in 1541. Fines of up to twenty shillings were payable by miscreants caught enjoying bowling and the lucrative statute was rigorously enforced.

By 1637 the Green was a ground 'where many gentlemen, with the gentile merchants of this town, take their recreation'. This photograph from 1894 shows the members, many of whom have their knighthood medals about their necks. The Knighthood of the Old Bowling Green Competition is the second oldest sports competition in the world, dating back to 1776.

When David Priestly won the tournament in 2009, he described it as being 'brilliant!' He was invested 'Sir' David, by 'Knight in Charge', 'Sir' Fred Rolfe, in the presence of the Sheriff of Southampton, Councillor Carol Cuneo, the Town Crier, John Melody and the 'Master of the Green', Alan Pickett. The photograph shows the current Knights of the Old Green, each proudly wearing their medals, which are engraved with the date they won the competition. Once a player has won the competition they can never play in it again. Front row: Sir Jim Barlow, 1985; Sir Fred Rolfe, Senior Knight, 1981; Alan Pickett, Master of the Green; Sir Michael Moore, 1989; Sir David George, 1996; Sir Les Fisher, 2001; Sir David Strickland, 2008. Back row: Vice Master Charles Matthews; Sir Martin Marum, 2002; Sir Graham Hart, 2003; Sir John Pleasant, 2006; Sir Donald Weaver, 2004.

THE SOUTHAMPTON PHILHARMONIC Choir began in an age when ladies were formally requested, in concert programmes, to 'conduce to the convenience and comfort of those sitting immediately behind them by removing their hats during the performance'. Originally known as the Southampton Sacred Harmonic Society, it was founded in 1860 and was conducted by Mr Alexander Rowland, RSM. It battled through the highs of celebrated performances and the lows of bankruptcy, held sales of work to bring in enough money to keep going and, eventually, was in a position to call for a high quality concert hall for Southampton, a call repeated regularly until the Guildhall was built in 1937.

The Southampton Philharmonic Society celebrates its 155th anniversary in 2015. This will be a double celebration as the choir's celebrated Musical Director, David Gibson, will celebrate twenty-five years with the choir in October 2015. This photograph was taken at the concert rehearsal in November 2009 at Winchester Cathedral, when a repertoire of Brahms, Haydn and Schubert displayed the choir's versatility.

6

MEN AT WORK

THIS 1910 PHOTOGRAPH from the Southampton Library's collection shows the site of what is now the West Quay shopping centre as it once was. The old indoor public baths and the Lido can be seen in the foreground. All of this would be built over during the twentieth century. *(With kind permission of Southampton Library)*

IN 1890 THE High Street was a much quieter place than it is now. This postcard shows just how elegant the street's buildings were before the Blitz destroyed so many of them.

Today, the Victorian High Street elegance can still be glimpsed but the road is increasingly utilitarian in the twenty-first century.

MR TYRRELL AND Mr Green opened their first 'high class' shop in Southampton in 1897. When Mr Tyrrell left the partnership Mr and Mrs Green continued trading, in larger premises in Above Bar (shown here in 1904) until they sold the business to the John Lewis Partnership in 1934. Despite being bombed in the Blitz, the company continued trading and rebuilt their premises after the war. By the late 1990s the premises were too small and so the shop was closed in 2000.

The business, now branded under the John Lewis name, took over state-of-the-art premises in the West Quay centre. The photograph on the left (below) shows the old Tyrrell and Green building in 2005. It was demolished in 2010 and today new offices, flats and restaurants are being built on the site.

(With kind permission of Southampton Library)

ALBERT ROAD WAS built in 1837 by the Floating Bridge Co. and was originally named Floating Bridge Road. Most of the street's original terraced housing was demolished in the 1960s. The image above shows some of the buildings near Elm Terrace in 1965, just before they were demolished.

This sad-looking boarded-up hotel below (left) was photographed in August 2005. It is impossible to find any trace of the Queen's Hotel in Albert Road now (right). Local residents think it was on this site, which has been sitting in this half-finished condition for several years.

(Photograph on left courtesy of Julie Green)

WEST QUAY UNDER construction in January 2005. Southampton seems to be in a permanent state of evolution, with building sites dotting the city.

The view of West Quay, below left, was looking across from the old Post House Hotel in 2005. You can see that there are vast tracts of land that are undeveloped, although the West Quay dual carriageway is as busy as ever.

Taken from the roof of the Holiday Inn, the image on the right shows that five years have made a bit of a difference. Carnival, the shipping line that now owns the Cunard brand name, has premises that now stand in front of the distinctive blue and yellow of the recent Scandinavian Ikea store. Carnival now obscures the multi-storey car park, which was at the centre of the earlier photograph.

7

OUT AND ABOUT

LONDON ROAD IN 1912 was starting to bustle, with shops lining the street, their canopies out to shield their wares from the sunshine, and the open-top tram travelling along the middle of the road.

MAYFLOWER MEMORIAL & TOWN QUAY,
SOUTHAMPTON.

DOCK WORKERS STREAM from the Town Quay on their bicycles in this 1930s postcard. There is so little traffic that they take up most of the road, making it difficult for the lone motorist in the background.

Today the bicycles are not in evidence but the motorists certainly are! The trees have moved back from the side of the road, replaced by bollards, but, apart from those changes, there seems little difference between the two images. Of course, there is no ship berthed at Town Quay as there was in the 1930s photograph and so no dockworkers.

(Photograph courtesy of Julie Green)

IN 2004 THE British Telecom building at the top of the High Street looked a sorry sight as it had been up for sale and was, at the time this photograph was taken, under offer.

By 2010 the office block was gone, replaced by residential apartment blocks with shops beneath. The heritage of the site lives on though, in the name of the doctor's surgery on the ground floor, Telephone House Surgery.

(Photograph courtesy of Zed Eric Malunat)

UPPER AVENUE AT the turn of the twentieth century was a peaceful place, with paths and unmade roads. This was the main entry into Southampton from Winchester, and the Cowherd's public house, just along the Avenue, would have been the first hostelry the weary traveller would come to. The elm trees were planted in 1745 and gave an impressive welcome into the town.

Today Upper Avenue is still a pretty place but much less impressive due to the sheer volume of traffic that thunders along the road. These days the paths and road are made up but trees are still in evidence along most of the road.

East Street, Southampton.

EAST STREET HAS always been a busy shopping street. It was the site of the original Marks and Spencer shop, which opened at 4 East Street in about 1910. In the distance in this shot is the clock over the Stanhope's Goldsmiths Co.

Today East Street is still a very busy shopping area, despite the recent demolition of the East Street Shopping Centre. This was the first of the indoor shopping centres in the town. It has been pulled down to make way for a major supermarket.

THE COMING OF the railway in 1840 and the growing importance of the docks brought the development of Oxford Street as an area for the middle classes. It was a business hub in the nineteenth century. This photograph shows the Sailor's Home on the right, which operated for over 100 years.

Today Oxford Street is a conservation area, filled with smart restaurants. The Sailor's Home is now the Booth Centre, a hostel for homeless men run by the Salvation Army.

RUMBRIDGE STREET, TOTTON, in 1908, looking towards Batts Corner. This used to be the main shopping street in Totton. Batts Corner is named after C.F. Batts who bought the two cottages on the corner where the High Street meets Rumbridge Street, Eling Lane and Junction Road. At this point, so the sign over the top of the combined building says, it is 77 miles to London and 24 miles to Bournemouth.

Today Rumbridge Street has an air of decline about it. The street looks run down and past its heyday, an image that the shuttered businesses do nothing to dispel. The Peg and Parrot pub now occupies the premises (Goddard's a century ago).

(With kind permission of Southampton Library)

EAST PARK TERRACE, seen above in 1930, was once a residential street dating from the 1850s. It was heavily bombed in the Second World War and the area was then used for education, being the site of the old Colleges of Art and of Technology.

The photograph below (left) was taken in 2005 by Jim Brown and shows an empty office block next door to the central ambulance station. Today (right) Southampton Solent University is the sole occupant of East Park Terrace. The rest of the area has been cleared, ready for the Terrace's next reincarnation.

ST MARY'S CENTRAL fire station was one of four stations operated by the Southampton Fire Brigade. This 1965 photograph shows two Bedford fire appliances, a Dennis and an AEC Turntable Ladder. St Mary's Road was the first purpose-built fire station and headquarters in Southampton and opened in 1909. It was demolished in 2000.

On 1 April 1974 the Southampton Fire Brigade was merged into the Hampshire Fire Brigade, which subsequently became the Hampshire Fire and Rescue Service. The new St Mary's fire station was occupied from December 2001 and officially re-commissioned on 27 March 2002, exactly ninety-seven years to the day that the original St Mary's fire station was opened. It incorporates a brass fireman's pole from the original 1909 fire station. The station now operates Volvo water tenders and a water-tender ladder.

THE ART HOUSE, which had been running as a commercial gallery for around two years, opened in January 2008 and was run as a not-for-profit café, gallery and venue. Within fourteen months the managers found that their lovely Grade II listed building on Bedford Place was just too small for all of the events they put on (people had started having to listen to poetry readings from the corridor).

The Art House moved to 178 Above Bar Street on 25 March 2009 and reopened a month later, going from strength to strength since then and bringing some art and fun to the emerging Cultural Quarter! Events cover sewing to seed banks, open mic poetry sessions to musical evenings. The Art House is the venue for Writing Buddies, the group for writers in Southampton. The photograph shows Nina Fraser, former Co-director of The Art House, with her beloved bicycle.

THIS VERY EARLY twentieth-century photograph shows Victoria Road, Woolston.

Today Victoria Road is fighting back from a decline during the recent recession and the number of empty shops is diminishing. Some of its earlier bustle is returning to the area.

WOOLSTON HAD ITS own fire station from 28 October 1929 until 17 January 1996. The advent of the Itchen Bridge allowed the quick transit of a fire appliance from one side of Southampton to another and it was decided that Woolston was no longer needed.

The station reopened as a doctor's surgery, The Old Fire Station Surgery, soon afterwards.

(Photograph above courtesy of Alan House, Hampshire Fire and Rescue Service)

THIS IS AN interesting study of Woolston from the crossroads between Portsmouth and Victoria Roads looking down towards the slipway. In the distance the floating bridges are mid-river, while in the foreground on the left a child plays with a hoop.

Now, the crossroads are traffic light controlled. It is just possible to glimpse the Itchen at the bottom of the hill. Today the crossroads is overlooked by the Millennium Feather, created by artist Peter Codling, the giant feather sculpture that was inspired by flight and sail, both of which Woolston has long connections with.

(Photograph courtesy Alan House, Hampshire Fire and Rescue Service)

ON 27 NOVEMBER 1959 there was a fire at 'H' warehouse, at the premises of Messrs Thomas Bros, upholsterers. This was the first time the Southampton Fire Brigade had used its new turntable ladder.

Today the warehouse still stands and is a restaurant, even though most of the rest of the warehouses in the area have been demolished. The St Mary's fire crew was happy to take a modern turntable ladder along to the site for this modern-day version of the photograph – without the fire!

(Photograph courtesy of Alan House, Hampshire Fire and Rescue Service)

THE SOUTHAMPTON FIRE Brigade Control Room was situated on the first floor of the St Mary's Road fire station. This 1946 photograph shows the telephone system and the telegraph receiving equipment for fire alarms located in the streets. This was operated by activating a clockwork switch located at intervals in the streets, which

relayed the location of the switch to the Control Room, whereupon a fire engine would be sent out to deal with the emergency. The person on the street who had activated the alarm would then point the Fire Brigade in the direction of the fire.

Today the Control Room for the whole of Hampshire is located at the Eastleigh headquarters. A light, bright, airy room, it is a stark contrast to its dark 1946 predecessor. Technology is still in evidence, although this is of the digital variety, not the mechanical of the 1940s.

8

NETLEY

THE ROYAL MILITARY Hospital at Netley was built to train army medical staff and to treat military patients. The aim was to return them to duty as quickly as possible. The site at Netley was chosen as it was close to Southampton, the port gateway to and from the British Empire. The high maintenance costs associated with keeping the hospital open led to its downfall. The hospital closed down in 1958, leaving just Albert House, the psychiatric hospital, open on the site. In June 1963 the empty building was badly damaged by fire and when the pipes burst during the winter of the same year, it was decided to demolish the once proud building. This started in 1966. Albert House remained open until 1978, when all medical activity on the site ceased. Now it is the Royal Victoria Country Park, the site having been bought by Hampshire County Council, in 1979. The Officers Mess was redeveloped into luxury flats and the chapel is now all that remains of the once proud hospital. *(Photograph courtesy of the Lingwood Netley Hospital Archive)*

(Photograph courtesy of the Lingwood Netley Hospital Archive)

Victoria Road, Netley.

3442.

THE FIRST THING that strikes you about this early twentieth-century photograph of Netley's main street is the lack of traffic. Apart from the children playing and housewives going about their business, the scene is peaceful and serene. With no street markings the slight incline up the road is not pronounced and the single street light must have cast a very meagre light indeed. The substantial villas are almost wholly obscured by large trees and it is difficult to believe that Britain's first general military hospital is just yards away behind the photographer. Opposite the houses, out of camera shot behind the trees, was Cliff House, which was visited by Queen Victoria in 1882.

The modern image shows how little the road itself has actually changed. The row of villas is still there, although some of the substantial boundary walls have been demolished to allow for parking in the premises' front gardens. Those that are left have all been painted black and white, giving a striking uniformity to the scene. The greenery has substantially diminished, allowing the twenty-first century audience to see the buildings now they are no longer hidden away. Opposite the villas flats now take the place of the old Cliff House. The most striking change is to the amount of traffic. It took many minutes of patient waiting to take a shot without a moving car in it.

(Photograph courtesy of the Lingwood Netley Hospital Archive)

THIS PHOTOGRAPH, OF the entrance to the Royal Military Hospital, Netley, dates from the beginning of the twentieth century. The gatehouse and guardhouse are both intact and the whole seems to offer an air of Victorian gentility. Note the park bench on the right foreground – it was fashionable to watch the action on Southampton Water as much then as it is now!

Today the gatehouse is still in place, now a private residence, but a lot has changed. The road is now made up with tarmac and yellow lines and wooden bollards give testament to the number of cars coming to the area. The hospital is now a public park, catering to the leisure needs of local people. It is a great place to walk a dog and get some fresh air. The park bench is still just outside the park entrance, but it has moved nearer the shore and is now out of camera shot. The area from the old park bench towards the photographer is now given over to car parking.

THE NETLEY MILITARY Cemetery lies behind the old Netley Hospital site in Cemetery Wood and contains the graves of those who died at the hospital. The cemetery opened in 1864. The War Memorial was unveiled in 1920 by General John (Jack) Seely, later the first Baron Mottistone (1868-1947), who had been Secretary of State for War immediately before the First World War. He commanded the Canadian Cavalry Brigade during the war, and was mentioned in dispatches five times for bravery. This early photograph shows many of the graves with simple wooden crosses, prior to receiving their stone memorials. There are 636 First World War British casualties buried in the military cemetery, as well as other nationalities, including sixty-nine German nationals who died in the same war. The cemetery is the property of the Ministry of Defence.

Today the Netley Military Cemetery, which closed to new burials in 1978, displays the uniform rows of white military headstones, which instantly identifies it as coming under the auspices of the Commonwealth War Graves Commission. Thirty-five Second World War dead are buried in the cemetery, which, in total, numbers 749 war casualties.

(Photograph courtesy of the Lingwood Netley Hospital Archive)

CEMETERY R.V. HOSPITAL NETLEY.

(Photograph courtesy of Netley Library – Hampshire County Library Service)

THE FOUNDATION STONE for Netley Abbey Infants School was laid in 1884 and it opened its doors to sixteen of the village's children on 13 April 1885. It had cost £850 to build. The first headmistress, Ms Edgington, came from Butlocks Heath School. Eighty-two children attended the school in the first year. According to Ken Ford in his *Netley Abbey Infants School 1884-1984*, the first children on the register are Minnie and Herbert Clatworthy,

who, he says, 'were probably first in the queue'. The youngest child who started school at Netley in 1885 was two years and two months, the oldest, seven years and seven months. Reading, writing and arithmetic were unsurprising choices on the syllabus, which also included singing, needlework and drawing. This photograph, taken inside the school in July 1919, shows the Peace Party, to celebrate the Armistice. Note the Union flag flying proudly from the cake on the desk to the far left. This was part of several celebratory events that took part in the village, which included a Peace Celebration Sports and also a Procession through the village on 19th July.

The school closed in 1984 and a branch library opened in the Old School building on 11 November 1986. County Councils had been granted the right to set up public libraries in 1921 and volunteers operated these, with stock from County Library Headquarters in Winchester. In May 1949 the Old Fire Station in New Road became a library with paid staff, but this building developed faults and was condemned in 1971. After that Netley had a mobile library service for fifteen years. The Old School building was converted at a cost of £55,000 with an additional £4,000 for shelving and furniture. Initially it was open for only eleven hours a week, which has gradually been extended over the years.

MISS MARGARET L. LORIMER was headteacher between 1923 and 1932. Here she is on the left, with Miss Edwards, her assistant, in 1928, standing in the doorway of the Station Road entrance. Note the tie around Miss Lorimer's neck and their drop-waisted dresses, typical of the period. They were both thoroughly modern misses! Ken Ford notes that when

Miss Lorimer took over her position she was very surprised to find that the lavatories had to be flushed from the headteacher's toilet. She was thus very conscientious in making sure that this was flushed at regular intervals!

Today the Hampshire County Library Service staff are in charge of the building and, as you can see, the doorway has not changed, although the door now has a letterbox and the entry to it has had to comply with

(Photograph courtesy of Netley Library)

disability laws and now has a ramp leading to it, as well as a flight of steps. Liz Ball, on the left, has worked at the library since 1986 and is the supervisor there now. She remembers the draught excluder being fitted to the bottom of the door. 'It was put on because there was such a gap under the door where the step had worn down.' Liz stands next to Linda Glasspool, assistant supervisor at Eastleigh, on temporary duty at Netley when the photograph was taken. These ladies wear typical twenty-first century attire: trousers, long skirts and boots have replaced the demure frocks of yesteryear.

BIBLIOGRAPHY

Books

Brown, J., *The Illustrated History of Southampton's Suburbs*, The Breedon Books Publishing Co. Ltd, 2004

Ford, K.A., *Netley Abbey Village in Old Picture Postcards*, European Library – Zaltbommel/Netherlands, 1992

Ford, K., *Netley Abbey Infants School*, Ken Ford, 1996

Gadd, E.W., *The Changing Face of Southampton*, Paul Cave Publications Ltd, 1981

Gallaher, T., *Southampton's Inns and Taverns*, Poulner Publishing Ltd, Ringwood, 1995.

Gallaher, T., *Southampton Events, People and Places over the 20th Century*, Sutton Publishing, 2000

House, A., *Serving the Community St Mary's Fire Station 1909 – 2000*, Alan House, 2000

House, A., The *Tradition Lives On – Recommissioning of St Mary's Fire Station 27 March 2002*, Alan House, 2002

King, R.G., *Itchen Ferry Village*, RG King, undated

Leonard, A.G.K., *Southampton*, (Vols one, two and three), Tempus Publishing Ltd, 1997, 2002 and 2006

Mitchell, V., and Smith, K., *Southern Mainlines Woking to Southampton*, Middleton Press, 1988

Rance, A., *Southampton Then and Now*, Milestone Publications, 1985

St Mark's Church Millennium Group, *Woolston Parish Past and Present*, St Mark's Church Millennium Group, 1999

Wheatley, K., *Marina Developments Limited so far ...* Marina Developments Limited, Southampton, 1997

Also: The 1961-1965 scrapbook in the archives of Southampton airport

Websites:

2nd Southampton Scouts: www.2ndsouthamptonscouts.co.uk

AB Ports: http://www.abports.co.uk

About Britain: http://www.aboutbritain.com

Assura: www.assuragroup.co.uk

Bank of England: http://www.bankofengland.co.uk

BBC: http://www.bbc.co.uk

Berkley Group: http://www.berkeleygroup.co.uk

Bio: http://bio.fsu.edu

Commonwealth War Graves Commission: http://www.cwgc.org

Christ Church: http://www.christ-church-freemantle.hampshire.org.uk

Culture 24: http://www.culture24.org.uk

Daily Echo: http://www.dailyecho.co.uk

David St John: http://www.davidstjohn.co.uk

Discover Southampton: www.discoversouthampton.co.uk

Don't Stay In: http://www.dontstayin.com

Gale and Polden: http://www3.hants.gov.uk

Geograph: http://www.geograph.org.uk

Girl Guides: http://www.girlguiding.org.uk

Hampshire County Council: www3.hants.gov.uk

Hampshire Police Band: www.hampshirepoliceband.co.uk

Hants Fire: www.hantsfire.gov.uk

Southampton Council: http://www.southampton.gov.uk/s-environment/public-art/pastprojects/feather.aspx

Holidays Guide: http://uk.holidaysguide.yahoo.com

Hythe Ferry: http://www.hytheferry.co.uk

John Lewis: http://www.johnlewis.com

Mayflower theatre: http://www.mayflower.org.uk

Medieval Archeology Volume 8 (Society for Medieval Archeology, 1964)

E Mentor and Company: http://www.photohistory-sussex.co.uk/BTNMentor.htm

Network Southeast Railway Society: http://www.nsers.org.uk/

Peartree Church: http://www.peartreechurch.org.uk/

Peter Gould's Local Transport History: www.petergould.co.uk

Plimsoll: http://www.plimsoll.org

Southampton Health: www.southamptonhealth.nhs.uk

Southampton Philharmonic Choir: www.southamptonphil.org

Southern Life: www.southernlife.org.uk

Southampton: http://www.southampton.gov.uk

Southampton Park Hotel: http://www.southamptonparkhotel.com/southampton-park-hotel.htm

Spartacus: http://www.spartacus.schoolnet.co.uk/PRpalmerston.htm

SS *Uganda*: http://www.ssuganda.co.uk/nevasa/index.html

The Art House: http://www.thearthousesouthampton.co.uk/index.htm

UK attractions: http://www.ukattraction.com/southern-england/museum-of-archaeology.htm

VT Group: http://en.wikipedia.org/wiki/VT_Group

Wikipedia: http://en.wikipedia.org

Zoo Chat: http://www.zoochat.com/1101/african-elephant-southampton-zoo-1981-a-64655/

Zoo directory: http://myweb.tiscali.co.uk/zoodirectory/closed.htm